Selling a Home through Probate:

How to Avoid Probate Pitfalls

David J. Delgado, SR

Selling a Home through Probate: How to Avoid Probate Pitfalls

Copyright © 2013 by David J. Delgado, SR

All rights reserved. No part of this book may be reproduced or transmitted in any form or by any means without written permission from the author.

Printed in USA by

ISBN-13:

978-1494380311

Table of Contents

Table of Contents	4
Introduction	5
Chapter One: Estate Planning	8
Chapter Two: Selling a Home through Probate	12
Chapter Three: How to Sell During Probate	16
Chapter Four: Issues to Avoid	25
Chapter Five: Strategies for Successful Outcomes	31
Chapter Six: How to Buy During Probate	34
Conclusion	36
Resources	40

Introduction

Everything You Need to Know About Probate

While nobody likes to think about it, we all die eventually. If you own your own home, it's important to know what will happen to it after you're gone. Legally the property has to be passed on to the people listed in the person's Will. Of course there isn't always a Will there to use as a reference. In these cases the people receiving assets will be designated by the State Law. So if you want a specific person to receive your estate, you need to put it in a Will. The process of selling the home after death is known as Probate.

Understanding the Probate process

The 'probate' process determines who gets the home and how it is sold. The entire process involves:

- The court appoints an executor to take over the deceased's affairs
- Heirs are found and identified
- The assets and property of the deceased are taken into account
- All debts owed will be paid off
- Estate tax returns will be filed and any taxes will be paid off
- Assets and property of the estate will be sold to pay taxes and bills of the estate
- The heirs will receive the remaining assets/property

This whole process can take anything from six months to four years to complete. It depends upon the State Laws and whether the home needs to be sold or not. There are also times when the heirs dispute what they are owed. If there are any problems then this will slow the process down.

Probate is an actual legal document that states who the executor is and it can be used in the court law if needed. If the state recognizes tenancy by the entireties for married couples, the spouse of the deceased will automatically receive a portion of the estate even if there isn't a Will.

The role of the executor

The executor is the only person who can legally deal with the estate of the deceased. They work in accordance to the Will and distribute the estate accordingly. If there isn't a Will an administrator rather than an executor takes over and the next of kin will usually receive the assets and estate.

The executor plays an important role in the distribution of the property. They need to work out the full value of the estate and everything it covers. One of the first jobs is to pay off any inheritance tax. When a person dies, their home is taxed before it is passed on to the heirs. The amount of tax charged on the property will vary depending upon its value. Basically the more the property is worth, the higher it will be taxed.

All debts are then paid off. It's actually quite a stressful job being an executor. Any mistakes made in the totaling of the assets and property will be blamed on the executor. For this reason they need to investigate everything thoroughly. They need to know how to fill out tax returns and court documents to have the probate granted. It's a tough job and they have to follow proper guidelines.

Is Probate always needed?

The only way to avoid the Probate process is to create a living trust before you die. This ensures the heirs chosen by the descendant receive the assets and property after death. The main reason people choose to create a living trust is because it isn't made public. A person's Will is made public so everyone can see what was left to whom and that can cause problems.

A living trust also mainly manages to avoid the probate process. It speeds up the transfer of the property and there may be some tax benefits. However, there are also down sides to this too. The cost is a major disadvantage. It's a lot more expensive to create a living trust than it is to create a Will.

The benefits of Probate

While it can take years to complete the entire Probate process, there are advantages of the system. When your loved one has passed away, the last thing you want to be worrying about is calculating their estate. The executor does all of the hard work for you. They sort out any debts that may need paying, they pay off the tax and they investigate everything for you.

Before a deceased's property is sold, it needs to have been granted Probate. It's not always made overly clear to potential buyers that the process can take years before the house can legally be theirs. This leads to frustration from all parties as the seller obviously wants the funds as quickly as possible and the buyer also wants to move into their dream home quickly.

Overall it's important to understand Probate if you're looking to buy or sell a property you've inherited. There are so many factors that need to be taken into account and it can be a really lengthy process.

Chapter One: Estate Planning

Estate Planning: Everything You Need to Know

Owning your own property comes with a wide range of responsibilities. One that you don't always think about is what will happen to it when you are no longer around. After you die, the property will usually go through the probate process. If you want to leave it to a particular person you'll need to make sure you've included it in your Will. Estate planning is something you can do before you die to ensure your loved ones get what they are owed.

What does estate planning involve?

Estate planning involves working out where you want your property and all of your assets to go once you die. When you mention the word 'estate' it's easy to assume it means the property alone. However, it can include all of the contents and any other assets you have including:

- Jewellery
- Clothes
- Cash
- Cars
- Land
- Furniture
- Investment, savings and retirement accounts
- Other houses

Estate is basically a collective term used to describe your entire belongings. As well as ensuring that certain things are left to the right people, estate planning can help you to save money on taxes too. It can also help to outline any guardians of children if it's needed.

Actual estate planning includes Wills, trusts and Power of Attorney. You need to appoint somebody you trust to be your Power of Attorney after you've gone. They basically help to ensure that your final wishes are kept.

Understanding estate taxes

Estate taxes are not to be confused with probate expenses. You can limit these taxes by creating a living trust. Final income taxes will need to be paid from any income you earned during the year that you die.

It is Federal estate taxes that tend to cause the most problems. They are notoriously high and can be as much as 45%-55%. What's more, they have to be paid off within nine months after you die, in cash. Most estates don't have this much cash available so numerous assets have to be liquidised to make up the money owed. If you plan ahead however, you can make sure your loved ones don't get stuck trying to pay off this tax.

If the estate is left to a Federal recognised charity or if it's left to a spouse, this form of tax won't usually apply.

It's worth noting that the estate tax laws will vary from state to state. Therefore you'll need to seek legal guidance in your own state if you want the most accurate picture of how much will be charged on your estate.

There are ways to lower or eliminate these taxes. Some people use life insurance plans to cover the money that gets paid out in taxes. This isn't always a great plan however. It can be good for those who are pretty wealthy. However, it doesn't always pay off so you do need to be careful if choosing this option.

A simpler method of lowering taxes from the estate is by removing certain assets before you die. This can include moving savings and other financial accounts into a loved one's account. The tax and fees will only be worked out based upon the assets that are in the property so the more you can eliminate the better. However, hiding the assets isn't necessarily the best idea. You could get found out and that would be a breach of the law. Therefore if you do plan on removing the assets, you need to make sure you are getting rid of them completely.

If you're married, it's possible you could use both exemptions to eliminate tax too. According to current laws, providing your spouse lives within the US, you can leave them any amount of money that you wish and it won't suffer estate taxes. However, when your spouse dies, it can cause a few problems. This is mainly true if the combined estate totals more than the exemption amount. Once the estate adds up to more than the exemption limit, the tax rates get ridiculously high. By using both exemptions via a living trust, the estate can be divided equally. This can save a lot of taxes in the long term.

Start planning your estate now

There are many things you need to be aware of when planning your estate. Start out by writing a list of assets and everything you own. Then work out if there are ways to lower your estate taxes if they apply. Create a Will to ensure that your loved ones get everything you want to leave to them.

It's not one of the happiest things to do, but planning your estate as early as possible can really help your loved ones after you've gone. There's so much that you don't often think about. The grieving process is hard enough so make it easier on the people you love by getting your affairs in order before the time comes.

Chapter Two: Selling a Home through Probate

There are a few key benefits to selling a house in probate. The first reason why you would sell in probate is to settle any liabilities. There are times when the deceased has left a number of liabilities behind such as taxes or debts. The payment for these liabilities may not be realized without liquidating assets from the estate of the deceased. In these cases, real estate offers a good method of settling the aforementioned liabilities through liquidation.

The second reason you would sell in probate is to offer monetary preference to the heirs. There may be many heirs and beneficiaries in the last will, but they may not want to take up the property as it is now. They may prefer to turn the real estate they inherited into the equivalent monetary value.

The third reason you would sell in probate is for the "no share, don't care" rule. Some wills have a provision for shared ownership of real property amongst heirs. However, some heirs would rather sell the real property at an undervalued price in lieu of sharing it with a fellow heir. Selling the house through probate is a great solution for this.

The next reason you would sell in probate is to avoid the cumbersome management of the property. Inherited property can be burdensome to manage due to possible renovation and repair costs, pending mortgage payments, or property taxes in accordance with state laws. By selling the house through probate, these long term issues can be avoided.

Of course, there is also avoiding the tragedy of loss. Many do not want to go through the belongings left behind by a loved one who recently passed, especially if they died in the house which was inherited. For this reason, many people would rather sell the house so that they can come to terms with the loss and move on forever.

It is also beneficial to sell through probate because it minimizes risks and losses. As aforementioned, it can become a liability more than an asset over the long term to care for a home you inherited. It makes sense to sell now rather than keep the property around as a risk factor if the repair and maintenance costs are increasing, or the house is losing value due to current market trends, or if it carries more risks and complications than it would were it to be liquidated.

Lastly, you may sell the property through probate as a testamentary requirement. Sometimes the deceased requires their property be sold in the last testament. This might be the case if the deceased wants to incorporate the funds from the sale into a trust for an heir, or to be shared among multiple beneficiaries, or to donate to a charity.

Whatever the reason for selling, it is the responsibility of the Executor of the estate to ensure the wishes of the deceased are enacted while simultaneously honoring probate laws.

The executor of an estate is not necessarily a lawyer or someone who has a legal background. In fact, an executor must meet only a few legal requirements. The first is that they are a legal adult in the state of the deceased's will. The second is that they have no criminal record.

Ideally, the executor is someone you can trust who is reliable and competent. It is also best if they had a personal relationship with the deceased before their death, and they have an understanding of the deceased's family. It is also important that they are willing to devote their time and energy to overseeing the actualization of the last wishes of the deceased.

The person who is named executor may not be able to serve when the deceased passed because they are disinterested, cannot afford the time required, predeceased the deceased, are ineligible due to state laws, or has been found by the courts to be unable to serve.

General Role of an Executor

The role of the executor is to inform all of the relevant parties about the deceased passing. This includes insurance companies, financial institutions, government institutions, utility providers, etc... They must then take inventory of all finances, possessions, and assets while also getting new appraisals for all valuables including jewelry, art collections, collectibles, and real estate. The executor must then determine whether the estate will go into probate and if it does, they must file the necessary documents. It is their role to identify non-probate property. They must also inform all heirs and all beneficiaries of their mention anywhere in the estate.

The executor must then secure any property and look after all belongings. They should consult with all heirs and beneficiaries on any important issues. After this they must collect any debt owed to the deceased and settle any credit owed by the estate. They must also file tax returns. Once this is done the executor can distribute assets in accordance with the last testament.

The next major role of the executor relates to selling a house in probate. Once the decision has been made to sell the property in probate it is the duty of the executor to obtain a current valuation of the house from an independent appraiser. Then they must file the petition to sell the probate house with the appropriate courts. Once confirmation from the probate court is received, the executor is granted either full authority or limited authority to carry out this transaction. They must compile all of the necessary documents which will be used in the sale of the house. This includes contracts and disclosures. After this it is the duty of the executor to find a real estate agent who will conduct the sale. They must agree to terms and conditions for the transaction after which the executor consults back and forth with all heirs and beneficiaries. They must report to the courts in order to finalize the sale where necessary. Then the executor must present all necessary documents and channel the funds back to the estate of the deceased once the sale has been finalized.

Chapter Three: How to Sell During Probate

When your loved one passes, they leave behind more than their family. They leave behind their property. Some people have a last will but others die intestate. This means they do not have a last testament. In both situations the property must be legally and officially reassigned to heirs or beneficiaries in accordance with the state laws and the will (where applicable). This legal process of Probate is extensive and covers the validity of the will and the reassignment of probate property.

Parties Involved

A probate sale involves not just the courts but the deceased's survivorship. The parties involved in this process include:

1) The executor.

This is the person who was named in the will or appointed by the probate court to fulfill all terms and conditions of the last testament and manage the estate. This includes overseeing the sale of the probate property. This is also called the personal representative.

2) The administrator

This is the individual who was appointed by the probate court to oversee the administration of the state in the event that the there was no will left by the deceased. The administrator can be appointed in the event that an executor was named in the will but they are unable or unwilling to carry out the management of the estate.

3) The survivors

The heirs and beneficiaries mentioned for inheritance or estate transfers will be present.

4) The attorney

This is the legal representative for the estate in probate court.

5) The selling agent

This can be the real estate agent who is responsible for selling the probate property.

6) The prospective buyers

These are the parties interested in purchasing the house.

7) The buying agent

This may be the representation for the prospective buyer.

Documentation

When selling a house in probate, you will need a lot of documentation. A lawyer or legal advisor can greatly assist in identifying all of the necessary documents.

Disclosure

Disclosure is one common aspect of selling a house in probate. It is the duty of the selling agent to present disclosure documents to the administrator or executor as well as the beneficiaries and heirs which highlights the role of the agent in the sale. The real estate agent is also responsible for openly disclosing all aspects of the house to all prospective buyers.

Some of the required disclosure documents include:

- Condition of the property
- House appraisal
- Property insurance
- Tax certification
- House price and interest rate
- Revocable clauses of the contract
- And more

Deadlines

There are multiple deadlines when it comes to selling a house through probate. There are court deadlines, tax deadlines, deadlines for creditors, deadlines for heirs, and deadlines for deposits from interested buyers. It is imperative to maintain a schedule of all deadlines.

Direction

The executor must abide by the direction of the court and the last testament. It is important to adhere to the probate laws of your state. It is for this reason that hiring an attorney or other legal counsel is highly recommended.

Dealer

When you are finally ready to sell the house, you must pick a dealer to handle the transaction. This might be a real estate agent or a real estate auctioneer. The agent will know current realty market trends and have better exposure to the market as well as target customers. A real estate agent may even have potential buyers in mind who are not but a phone call away. The real estate agent of your choosing will aggressively market your probate house so that it gets the most competitive offers. They will use every medium of advertisement available including:

- Realty directory listings
- Online advertising
- Notices in dailies
- Signs
- And open house dates for show

Once your real estate agent has interested buyers they can set up appointments and guide them through the property personally.

A real estate auctioneer is another person who can get competitive pricing for your probate property at an auction.

Whichever option you choose, you must file documentation with the probate court so that you can obtain release forms and approval documents.

Duration

The time period required to sell a house through probate can take months and sometimes years. A swift sale IS possible so long as there are no objections by heirs or beneficiaries and no legal issues. The duration of this process is dependent upon:

- The amount of time it takes the executor or administrator to get court approval and title to sell
- The cooperation of beneficiaries and heirs
- The complexity of the estate
- The complications in settling taxes, debts, and other liabilities
- The intricacies of the asset division

Steps for Selling Property in Probate

Probate laws differ by state so it is important to familiarize yourself with your particular state laws before selling a home in probate. However, there are some general steps that you can take.

If the case is a testate case, the court will appoint an executor. In an intestate case, the court will assign an administrator.

After this the executor or administrator must get an appraisal for the property from an appraiser who has been approved by the state. This person will offer an independent valuation for the property as well as an appropriate list price.

Once this has been done a petition for the sale of the probate property must be filed with the court, which seeks to monetize the property either through a real estate agent or a property auction.

After this, the executor or the administrator must acquire a court order which approves the sale of the property. The court order will give the executor or administrator either limited powers or full powers to oversee the sale.

The executor or administrator will need to draft all necessary disclosure documents as well as contracts to present to the prospective buyers and to be used in court when the sale is finalized.

If there is a real estate agent, then the house will be listed in the existing market, advertised, and set for viewing by the agent by all interested buyers. The agent should find and meet buyers who have offers relevant to the list price and not any less than 90% of the property valuation. If there is a real estate auctioneer instead, a date should be set for auction and official notices should be relayed to the public in order to alert interested bidders.

Once this is done, the agent or auctioneer will enter into an agreement with the best buyer ("best" here is the buyer with the best offer against the list price of the property). The buyer will sign the contract which states that the sale is not final, but that it is bound to a court hearing and is dependent upon the decision of the probate court. After all buyer eventualities have been dealt with, an official notice will be given to all of the concerned beneficiaries and heirs which informs them of the offer and proposed terms which were agreed upon by the buyer and executor or administrator. The heirs and beneficiaries can either agree to all terms or object to all terms.

It is at this point that the sale will go in one of multiple directions.

If the executor or administrator has full authorization from the court:

- A notification of the sale and the offer from the buyer will be made public
- Any bidders who offer a higher amount will come forth.
- A court hearing can be filed by the executor or administrator
- If the executor or administrator opts out of the court hearing, and all parties agree to the terms for the sale,

then the deal can be closed in accordance with the "how" and "when" provisions of the last testament.
- If the executor or administrator opts to go to probate court to finalize the sale, the procedure is as follows:
    - The court is petitioned for a hearing wherein the deal must be signed and approved
    - The hearing date will be set based on the court's schedule
    - The prospective buyer will make a deposit of 10% of their offer before the scheduled court hearing
    - The executor or administrator must make a public notice for the proposed offer and sale, allowing any other interested buyers to join the bidding process in court
    - If there are additional buyers, another court date is set
    - The bidders must be made aware that:
        - They should know the condition of the property before hand
        - They must instantly submit a 10% deposit through a cashier's check to the court
        - The winner's 10% deposit is non-refundable once the court approves the sale
        - The original buyer who put down a deposit will get a refund if the sale is given to a higher bidder. But if they win, their deposit amount goes toward the agreed upon amount in court. For example: The original buyer bid for $50,000 and paid a 10% deposit on that of $5,000. But there were higher bids and the sale went to probate court where the original buyer out bid the

other buyers at a final rate of $60,000 for the house. That means the new deposit amounts to $6,000 and the original buyer who put down $5,000 owes the court an additional $1,000 immediately.
- Bidding in court will begin with the initial value of the property and progress in incremental amounts based on the state laws.
- The selling price must be no less than 90% of the valuation of the property, as set forth by an independent appraiser

If the executor or administrator has limited authorization from the court:

- The court is petitioned for a hearing wherein the deal must be signed and approved
- The hearing date will be set based on the court's schedule
- The prospective buyer will make a deposit of 10% of their offer before the schedule court hearing
- The executor or administrator must make a public notice for the proposed offer and sale, allowing any other interested buyers to join the bidding process in court
- If there are additional buyers, another court date is set
- The bidders must be made aware that:
  - They should know the condition of the property before hand
  - They must instantly submit a 10% deposit through a cashier's check to the court

23

- The winner's 10% deposit is non-refundable once the court approves the sale
- The original buyer who put down a deposit will get a refund if the sale is given to a higher bidder. But if they win, their deposit amount goes toward the agreed upon amount in court. For example: The original buyer bid for $50,000 and paid a 10% deposit on that of $5,000. But there were higher bids and the sale went to probate court where the original buyer out bid the other buyers at a final rate of $60,000 for the house. That means the new deposit amounts to $6,000 and the original buyer who put down $5,000 owes the court an additional $1,000 immediately.
- Bidding in court will begin with the initial value of the property and progress in incremental amounts based on the state laws.
- The selling price must be no less than 90% of the valuation of the property, as set forth by an independent appraiser

Chapter Four: Issues to Avoid

As an executor selling a house through probate you will face a myriad of potential issues.

Issue #1: Size

The first issue is the size of the probate estate. The size of the property is directly proportional to the amount of work the executor will face. Probate estates which have been valued in the millions require additional help in terms of auditing and valuation.

How to overcome this?

Make sure to hire professional auditors to help complement the role as executor. Before the executor accepts the role, it is important to determine the size of the estate so there are no shockers when it comes time to get down to work.

Issue #2: Additional Expenses

One of the biggest fears held by an executor is the fiduciary responsibility they have (or financial liability). When selling a house through probate there are many expenses incurred. These additional expenses should be funded from the estate, which can be quite a burden. In terms of additional expenses, at the top of the list are lawyer fees.

Most likely, legal counsel will be required for the estate administration. There may be federal or state tax laws which require an attorney. There may be issues with joint ownership over the probate house, and the other party may not agree to sell. This requires an attorney. One beneficiary may contest the will in probate court, in which case the house cannot be sold until it is settled. This may require an attorney. There may be legally binding contracts on the real estate in which the deceased entered years ago, which may require an attorney.

As you can see, there are a multitude of potential situations which will require an attorney and rack up a heavy list of fees.

Another source of additional fees is documentation. There is a lot of paperwork involved in selling a house through probate at the court level, state level, and federal level, all of which will require money. For example, the house cannot be sold without an official death certificate. This costs money for every official copy you need. While it is not a huge amount of money, it will add up nonetheless.

There may be additional fees for overhead costs such as repairs, state taxes, maintenance, insurance payments, mortgage funding, or appraisal fees before you can sell the house. There could be fees for dealers given that most cases involve a real estate agent. The real estate agents are paid either on a fixed amount agreed upon ahead of time or as a percentage of the selling price.

Lastly, there are probate court fees. Fees for probate court may amount to only ten or twenty dollars for each filing or document, but this will add up quickly as you have to pay for new applications, hearings, petitions, and more.

The fees for probate are often grouped into the following categories:

1. Service provision fees
2. Case processing fees
3. Legal copy fees

How to overcome this?

The executor should find out what anything and everything will cost. It is important to avoid spending what should not be spent, as the executor is accountable for anything spent by the estate. It is important to keep records of all expenditures, especially if a party to the estate or a court of law decides to challenge accountability of the executor. The executor should also research every required expenditure and leave anything for which they are not absolutely qualified to someone who is qualified.

Issue #3: Dissatisfaction from Heirs and/or Beneficiaries

The situations which could bear dissatisfaction from heirs and/or beneficiaries are countless. This remains the most overbearing challenge an executor will face. There could be endless possibilities for tension among heirs and beneficiaries including jealousy or rivalry. When selling a house in probate, the most common reasons for disagreement among heirs and beneficiaries include whether or not ownership should be shared, whether or not the house should be sold, the cost at which the house should be sold, who will get what percentage of returns after the sale, and how long it should take to sell the house.

How to overcome this?

An executor should always check with beneficiaries and heirs and let them know why you are doing something, when it will be done, how it will be done, and what you are specifically doing. The same is true of what you can do, what you should do, what you can't do, what you won't do, and what you shouldn't do. The executor is responsible (read: liable) for any steps taken so the reasoning for each action should be easily explained and justified to a court of law and to heirs. It is also important to remember that the heirs are people too. They will not be incredibly graceful at all times, especially since they are emotionally aggrieved and heartbroken; have some compassion and understanding as an executor but also be executive and decisive. The executor must remember their representation: what or who does the executor stand for? Why were they selected as executor in the first place? Recalling the answer to both is quite helpful when making decisions.

Issue #4: Finding Buyers and Good Prices

Buyers are often told to steer clear of probate houses due to the slew of paperwork, the court hearings, the non-refundable deposit on site, and the fact that not all issues may be disclosed before the property is purchased. But there are those who know that good deals are to be found among probate properties which is a good selling point for executors who want to sell a property quickly.

Finding a good buyer and finding a good price are both difficult. It is hard to get a good price because the majority of probate houses do not have time to sit on the market long enough to get the best price because heirs and probate courts often want it done NOW. This often results in executors settling for a price that "isn't too bad". In addition, many buyers would rather commit to a smaller price at the start of the sale because there is no guarantee with probate houses that their accepted offer will be accepted by the courts. They could go to court and bid on the probate house and still not get it. It is because of this that many buyers are not willing to write a particularly large check.

How to overcome this?

Go a little higher in price than you think it is worth. With a slightly unrealistic price, know that prospective buyers will undercut the list price; therefore their undercut rate won't be much lower than your expected value. It is also easier to reach your desired value when you place higher value on the house initially. Do not feel guilty about this either; business is business and taking a loss is NOT an option.

Issue #5: Time

Selling a house in probate is complicated and governed by the probate courts. The amount of time required to sell the house in probate can be lengthened if the executor is only given limited power versus full authority to process the sale. It is important to be psychologically prepared for this process to take well over a few months and possibly a year before all is said and done.

How to overcome this?

Make sure to disclose the nature of the transaction to all parties. Protect yourself as the executor from liability by giving every buyer a contract that contains full disclosure. Make sure you have a projected schedule for the selling process so that time is not wasted.

Chapter Five: Strategies for Successful Outcomes

Making improvements to the property

One of the key disadvantages many probate properties have is being a little old fashioned. The houses tend to be older, which means they aren't always in the best condition. Of course this isn't always the case, but it is quite common. No matter how old the property is, there's likely some changes that could be made to make it more investable. Consider sending all old furniture to auction. That way when potential buyers view the home, they won't be put off by drab looking furniture.

Any personal touches need to be removed from the property. Buyers are looking for a blank canvas. They need to be able to see themselves living in the property. It's essential to remove the personality of the previous owner before you list the property for sale.

Of course it's also important to make any repairs if needed. Absolutely anything you can afford to do to improve the property you should do. The only thing to keep in mind if you do make improvements to the home is that it could affect the probate. If the house value increases, you could end up having to pay more tax or other fees.

Seeking legal guidance

There will be a lot of paperwork that you need to fill out when selling through probate. It's highly recommended that you get legal help with this. They will be able to look over the documents and ensure you're filling them in correctly in accordance with the courts. It can be quite complicated filling in legal paperwork when you've no idea what you're doing. Don't do it alone when you really don't have to.

Investing in the services of a real estate agent

One of the easiest ways to sell the property is by using the services of a professional estate agent. They will have dealt with probate properties many times in the past. This means they know exactly how to market the property and what to expect. They will also have likely come across many potential problems in the past, which makes them ideal for handling any issues that may pop up.

Real estate agents are fantastic for marketing the property too. It's worth keeping in mind that the cost of selling a probate property shouldn't incur any additional charges over a standard sale. So when choosing a real estate agent, avoid ones that tell you the fees will be higher.

The real estate agent can drive in the right target market for the home too. This increases the chances that you'll sell it quite quickly. It's important to note that not all real estate agents are trustworthy. Some are only in it for the money and they won't take your best interests into account. For that reason it's important you compare the different agents available and choose the one with the best reputation and who you feel comfortable with after they show you proof of recent closed transactions. Before you interview a real estate agent, having a list of questions to ask for the interview process. Industry experts have put together 10 of the best questions to ask a real estate agent before you sign any agreement. To get a free copy of the 10 best questions call toll free 800-270-9096 enter ID 1084. The report will be mailed to you free of charge and no obligation.

Dealing with disputes quickly

Sometimes there may be family disputes that need to be sorted out. If the property was left to one sibling over another, it can cause problems. Perhaps the other sibling is contesting that they should be given the right to live in the house? The longer disputes go on, the more it will end up costing you. It's important to sit down with other members of the family until you can come to an agreement. Perhaps give them the chance to buy the house at the market value?

Overall selling a property through probate can be a stressful process. It can be made more bearable however if you use professional services such as a real estate agent.

Chapter Six: How to Buy During Probate

Properties can be sold in probate court at a lower price than other homes on the market. Homes sold in probate court are done so when someone dies without bequeathing property or dies intestate. At this point, the state will take over and administer the sale of the property. Probate laws vary by state, but each state wants to ensure the property is marketed and sold at a fair price.

The property in a probate sale is marketed the same as any other property. The probate attorney or the estate representative will hire an agent and sign a listing agreement. Then the property is shown the same as a traditional listing.

The price for a probate property is often based on the suggestion of the listing agent in conjunction with an independent appraisal as ordered by the court.

How to Make an Offer

Anyone interested in making an offer on a probate property must make an offer the same as a traditional property, but they must also offer a 10% deposit too. The sale is accepted or denied by the estate representative the same as any other sale.

The offer you place is subject to confirmation by the court. Just because the seller accepted the offer does not mean the seller is committed to the offer. The estate representative must petition the court for the sale. At this point a future date will be chosen to confirm the sale in court.

Once the sale date has been issued, all parties must wait between 30 and 45 days. In order to confirm the sale, the court will take the price offered by the buyer and increase by, say 5% in the state of California, and place the home back on the market. If any other buyers are interested, they, and the initial buyer, will come to court and the property will be sold in the form of an auction. The opening bid will be the original bid amount from the first interested party and then it will increase by, again, for example 5% in the state of California. If no other bidders show up to court then the property is given to the original buyer at their original offer. Once the property is sold, 10% must be handed over immediately. Many times this deposit is non-refundable.

Also, given that the seller is deceased, there is not often anyone to disclose aspects of the house which might negatively affect the value such as leaky windows or illegal work done to the property. Interested parties must conduct property inspections themselves before they write an offer.

Conclusion

Overall the process of selling a home after probate isn't always as straight forward as it could be. There are many pitfalls that you could fall victim to; especially if this is your first time dealing with an inherited property. There's so much that you need to think about. First things first, before you can sell the home it needs to go through the probate process.

When a loved one dies, their property needs to be passed on legally through the probate system. An executor is hired to take care of the process providing there's a Will. The Will basically shows who gets the assets and property now that the person has passed away. Any debts that they may have owed, plus any inheritance tax will need to be deducted from the property value.

Sometimes it makes more sense to sell the property, rather than to hang onto it. You also might not be in a position to keep the home anyway. If you're looking to sell through probate, there are a number of things you need to keep in mind. It's not a simple, straight forward process so it is advisable to seek help where you can.

Make sure to plan.

The process of probate and selling a home through probate can quickly become a complicated one for your heirs and your executor if you do not take the necessary steps now to ensure your assets and affairs are in order and your will is properly filed with the courts. By taking the extra steps to ensure things are handled now you can reduce the pressure on the backs of your loved ones and hopefully circumvent any fighting among heirs or beneficiaries after you pass.

1) Ask yourself if you have a will.

If you do not have a will to properly dispose of your assets upon death, then your estate will be distributed based on state intestacy laws. Wills are responsible for more than appointing a representative and disposing of your property. They also address trusts and guardians for minors, allocation of martial trusts, estate taxes, charitable bequests, as well as bond requirements and compensation for and authority to the personal representative who will sell your real estate assets.

After you have completed your will, you will need to inform your attorney as well as those who are appointed personal representatives (and any alternatives). At the time of death the original will has to be presented to Probate Court. If every intestate heir and testate heir agrees that the original will has been lost then a copy can be presented to Probate Court. If the will is maintained inside of a safe deposit box, the personal representative must legally have access to that safe deposit box for the purpose of retrieving the will.

2) Make sure you have Durable Power of Attorney

This is a powerful tool meant to appoint an agent to act on your behalf. The document gives the agent broad or limited power. A Durable Power of Attorney needs to be filed in your Register of Deeds office for your country of residence. Any accounts which are set up for the Power of Attorney should be separate and not any form of a joint account with the right of survivorship. The account should be titled, for example, "John Jacobs by Mary Jacobs as POA" in lieu of "John Jacobs and Mary Jacobs".

You must clearly state the authority of the POA to act on behalf of the principle. The powers you give might include the power to buy and sell property, the power to file tax returns, the power handle banking transactions, the power to settle claims, or the power to apply for government benefits. The power of gifting must also be directly addressed in the document, if you so choose.

If you fail to have a Durable Power of Attorney, no one will be placed in charge of your affairs and the family will have to petition in Probate Court while the courts appoint someone to manage your assets.

3) Make sure you have Health Care Power of Attorney

This will give someone the authority to make health care decisions on your behalf if you are mentally incompetent, unconscious, or otherwise unable to make your own decisions. If you fail to do this, there will be no one designated to make decisions for you and the Court will have to appoint a guardian. A copy of this form should be taken with you to the hospital each time you go and should also be sent to your medical providers and your named agent.

4) Make sure you have a Living Will

This will address two possible medical situations during the dying process. If two physicians declare you terminal or that you will die within a short time period, this document can give someone else the authority to turn down continued life support or execute continued life support. Again, each time you visit the hospital a copy of this form should be taken with you and one should be mailed to all of your medical providers.

5) Make sure you address your estate taxes.

If you calculate your rough estate tax amount you can reduce it before you pass by setting up gift plans or using a credit shelter that is tax free.

Resources

Some states do not have complete probate court systems while others have a thorough probate court system. You can look for your specific state laws on the following sites:

- EstateFinance.com - State Probate Laws
- FindLaw.com – Estate & Probate State Laws
- ProbateEstate.org – Probate Requirements by State

Additional resources to help answer any probate questions you may have:

- IRS.gov - Probate Proceedings
- EstateSettlement.com - Probate FAQs
- RealEstateLawyers.com – Probate Real Estate Investing
- FastProbatePropertySales.com – IAEA
- DavidDelgadoRealty.com – Selling Real Property During Probate

www.ingramcontent.com/pod-product-compliance
Lightning Source LLC
Chambersburg PA
CBHW070720180526
45167CB00004B/1554